Intersections:
Where Faith and Life Meet

A Cumberland Presbyterian
Adult Resource
Volume 8, Wisdom

Discipleship Ministry Team
Ministry Council
Cumberland Presbyterian Church

8207 Traditional Place
Cordova, Tennessee 38016

First Edition 2015

Published by The Discipleship Ministry Team
General Assembly Ministry Council of the Cumberland Presbyterian Church
Cordova, Tennessee

ISBN-13: 978-0692482988

ISBN-10: 0692482989

We want to hear from you.
Please send your comments about this curriculum to
the Discipleship Ministry Team at chm@cumberland.org.

OUR UNITED OUTREACH
Made Possible In Part By Your Tithe To Our United Outreach

Table of Contents

Editor: Cindy Martin
Designer: Joanna Wilkinson
Proofreader: Mark Taylor

To order, call 901-276-4572, x 252 or e-mail resources@cumberland.org.

The Wisdom Of Conflict

Scripture for lesson:
Judges 4:4-9, 14-15

Written by Tiffany Hall McClung

I have a friend who avoids conflict like the plague. If she believes asking for a lunch break away from the university campus where she works will mean having a difficult conversation with her boss, she avoids the conversation and sneaks around to take her lunch break. She hopes that no one will notice she was ever gone. Of course, someone always notices, and what could have been a mildly uncomfortable conversation becomes something much worse. Avoiding a perceived conflict rarely brings peace.

Prep for the Journey

Judges provides a snapshot of the Old Testament nation of Israel. God would provide a strong leader who followed God and led the people to follow God as well. The people knew peace and freedom during those times. Eventually, however, the leader either died or strayed from God's ways, and then the people forgot about God. During those times, they would be conquered by oppressors. When the people finally repented and returned to God, God would raise up a leader. This cycle repeated itself throughout the Old Testament. At this point in our passage, they had endured twenty years of persecution.

Read Judges 3:1-4.
Now these are the nations that the Lord left to test all those in Israel who had no experience of any war in Canaan ² (it was only that successive generations of Israelites might know war, to teach those who had no experience of it before): ³ the five lords of the Philistines, and all the Canaanites, and the Sidonians, and the Hivites who lived on Mount Lebanon, from Mount Baal-hermon as far as Lebo-hamath. ⁴They were for the testing of Israel, to know whether Israel would obey the commandments of the Lord, which he commanded their ancestors by Moses.

How do you deal with conflict? What changes would make your approach more effective? Where might you find wisdom in conflict?

Compare your faithfulness to that of God's. In what ways have you fallen away from God only to discover that God remains constant and always near?

Although Israel was under the rule of outside oppressors, God provided them with a series of leaders whom we know as the judges. Some of the more familiar judges include Deborah, Gideon, and Samson.

Read Judges 4:4-5.

At that time Deborah, a prophetess, wife of Lappidoth, was judging Israel. ⁵ She used to sit under the palm of Deborah between Ramah and Bethel in the hill country of Ephraim; and the Israelites came up to her for judgment.

Deborah made herself available to the people by "holding court" under a tree in a public, easily accessible area. The people of Israel saw something special in Deborah. They trusted her enough to bring their deepest hurts and most difficult decisions to her.

Some scholars think that the comment *wife of Lappidoth* could also be translated as "woman of fire." Perhaps this description was accurate in that she recognized the wisdom of the Holy Spirit and boldly followed the Spirit's leading.

Deborah was the last judge, it seems, who truly looked out for the Israelites and sought to discern God's wisdom. Gideon marked a change toward a downward spiral in the history of the judges, which was filled with selfish ambition and a growing unfaithfulness to God.

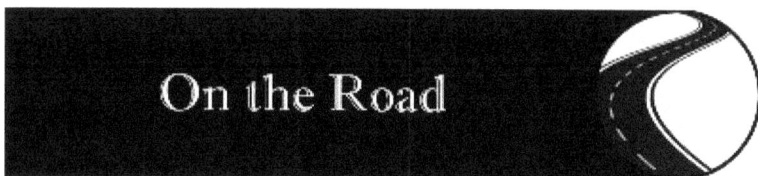

On the Road

Deborah was a prophet, judge, and military leader—one of only three about whom the Bible tells us. Moses and Samuel were the other two. Not only did the people trust her as a judge and leader, but they also trusted her to lead them into battle. If Deborah was willing to go into battle, they felt that God would be with them.

Read Judges 4:6-9, 12-15.

She [Deborah] sent and summoned Barak son of Abinoam from Kedesh in Naphtali, and said to him, "The Lord, the God of Israel, commands you, 'Go, take position at Mount Tabor, bringing ten thousand from the tribe of Naphtali and the tribe of Zebulun. ⁷I will draw out Sisera, the general of Jabin's army, to meet you by the Wadi Kishon with his chariots and his troops; and I will give him into your hand.'" ⁸ Barak said to her, "If you will go with me, I will go; but if you will not go with me, I will not go." ⁹ And she said, "I will surely go with you; nevertheless, the road on which you are going will not lead to your glory, for the Lord will sell Sisera into the hand of a woman." Then Deborah got up and went with Barak to Kedesh. ...

Why do you think it is significant that Deborah "held court" under a tree in a public space?

At what points in your life has God lifted up leadership to bring you back on track? Where do you find the most peace in your life with God?

What might Deborah have experienced in coming to the decision to lead Barak into battle? How do you make difficult decisions that affect others?

What helps you to discern God's will and direction?

Who are the people with power, wealth, and strength in our current culture? How are they oppressors? liberators?

When do you flee from confusion? What causes you to panic? How does the assurance of God's presence comfort you in those times?

[12] When Sisera was told that Barak son of Abinoam had gone up to Mount Tabor, [13] Sisera called out all his chariots, nine hundred chariots of iron, and all the troops who were with him, from Harosheth-ha-goiim to the Wadi Kishon. [14] Then Deborah said to Barak, "Up! For this is the day on which the LORD has given Sisera into your hand. The LORD is indeed going out before you." So Barak went down from Mount Tabor with ten thousand warriors following him. [15] And the LORD threw Sisera and all his chariots and all his army into a panic before Barak; Sisera got down from his chariot and fled away on foot.

During this time, Deborah received instructions from God that helped her to discern a way the Israelites could confront the oppressive Canaanite army and seek freedom. Following these instructions meant willingly entering into a conflict with Sisera, the commander of Jabin's army. Deborah knew the perfect person for the job: Barak.

Barak agreed to lead the Israelite army of 10,000 soldiers into this conflict, but only if Deborah would go as well. Together they led the Israelites into the Kishon Valley, where they defeated Sisera's army, which included "900 chariots of iron."

Any time scripture mentions something as specific as the 900 chariots of iron, it is a hint to pay attention and read between the lines. In this case, we are to understand that the army of Sisera was not only made up of many soldiers, but it was also powerful. The country's wealth allowed the army to have what we might consider state-of-the-art equipment. While the Israelites may have had 10,000 soldiers to fight in this conflict, they willingly went into a battle that they were unlikely to win against such a force of power, wealth, and strength.

Scenic Route

We can only imagine the confusion of a battle of this magnitude. Hundreds of horses and chariots charging, and thousands of soldiers engaging in hand-to-hand combat only added to the panic God brought upon the enemy army. It might have even been difficult to determine foe from friend. It must have been too much for Sisera, the commander, as he left his chariot and fled.

Read Judges 4:17-22.

Now Sisera had fled away on foot to the tent of Jael wife of Heber the Kenite; for there was peace between King Jabin of Hazor and the clan of Heber the Kenite. [18] Jael came out to meet Sisera, and said to him, "Turn aside, my lord, turn aside to me; have no fear." So he turned aside to her into the tent, and she covered him with a rug. [19] Then he said to her, "Please give me a little water to drink; for I am thirsty." So she opened a skin of milk and gave him a drink and covered him. ²⁰ He said to her, "Stand at the entrance of the tent, and if anybody comes and asks you, 'Is anyone here?' say, 'No.'" ²¹ But Jael wife of Heber took a tent peg, and took a hammer in her hand, and went softly to him and drove the peg into his temple, until it went down into the ground—he was lying fast asleep from weariness—and he died. ²² Then, as Barak came in pursuit of Sisera, Jael went out to meet him, and said to him, "Come, and I will show you the man whom you are seeking." So he went into her tent; and there was Sisera lying dead, with the tent peg in his temple.

The story becomes quite gory when we learn that Jael, the wife of a friend of King Jabin, welcomed the fleeing Sisera into her tent. Because he knew that she was a friend of the king, he accepted her offer of refuge, believing that her tent was a safe place to hide until he could return to Canaan. In fact, he felt safe enough that he fell soundly asleep. Jael then took a tent spike and drove it into his head, killing him. If we had not already felt squeamish with what appears to be God-ordained war, this part of the story puts too fine a point on it. (Pun intended!)

Jael was the third member of the team in this period of Israelite history. She joined Deborah and Barak as an essential person in defeating the Canaanites and bringing peace to the land. The forty years of peace that followed these events would not have been possible without Jael. We know she was important because we know her name, her history, and her actions. She is one of nineteen women characters about which the Book of Judges tells. This number is the most female characters mentioned in any book in the Bible.

Jael was from the Kenite clan. The word *Kenite* means "smith," which probably indicates that Jael and her husband were part of a nomadic clan of blacksmiths. As such, they would have maintained relationships with many of the various tribes and countries of that time by not taking sides.

When Sisera went to Jael for help—because he knew of her husband's loyalty—she had a difficult decision to make. She knew that Sisera's army had been defeated, which meant that the Israelites would look for and soon find Sisera. She also knew that if it appeared she was protecting their enemy, she and her entire family would suffer severe consequences. We can only speculate about her motives, but this situation was undoubtedly a difficult spot in which to find herself. She decided to kill Sisera and stand with the Israelites.

Why do you think it is important to know that Jael drove a tent peg through Sisera's head? Why do you think the writer included this information?

Who are the important women in the history of your congregation? How have they affected your faith journey?

When have you been caught between opposing forces? How did you ultimately choose the one with whom you would align yourself? What would have happened if you had remained neutral?

What are we to do with scripture that seems to be telling us that God called Deborah to lead the Israelites into a battle that would cause the death of so many Canaanites? How do we reconcile the worship of a Christ who is known as the Prince of Peace, with a horrific scene of murder? How do we answer all the questions that scriptures like these raise? Unfortunately, there are no easy answers, and our questions will likely remain unanswered. We could attempt to simplify God's ways to something that we might be able to imagine ourselves doing, but that would be a futile exercise. Our ways are not God's ways, nor can we possibly understand God's ways.

What we can discern from scriptures is that some conflict is unavoidable. Deborah saw a way to lead her people toward peace, but the path to peace meant taking some non-peaceful actions. However, Deborah, in her wisdom, understood that avoiding conflict would not bring about peace. On the contrary, avoiding conflict often causes it to escalate. Not only did Deborah's plan work, but it brought peace to that land for forty years.

Leaders often get caught between opposing groups. Although they may not side with one group over another, the perception can often be different than reality. Talk together about some ways you and your community of faith can keep these types of situations from occurring.

Consider some ways as a community to thank your leaders. It is often a tough and lonely job!

What are your thoughts about scriptures that seem to say God calls people to violence? How do you reconcile those thoughts with a savior who teaches us to love one another?

When has a conflict within your community of faith escalated due to avoidance of the issue? Speak honestly with one another about any such situations. Work together to discern the best path to long-term peace.

In the Rear View

Deborah was a woman with many gifts. It's safe to assume she was a fair and wise judge because the people came to her with their issues and concerns. Her prophetic gift manifested itself as she brought God's instructions about going to battle. She was a strong leader, as evidenced by her leading of Barak's army against the Canaanites.

Discernment was clearly a part of Deborah's wisdom. Take a few minutes as a group to reflect on the ways in which you believe Deborah was able to discern a plan that would lead to forty years of peace.

If you have time, reflect as a class on the violence in these passages, throughout the Bible as a whole, and in our own culture today. Could Deborah have achieved peace without violence?

How effective do you think individual discernment is? What does community discernment look like?

Travel Log

Day 1:

    With a 24/7 news cycle and members of congress who refuse to work together, conflict in our culture is front and center. But these "talking heads" yelling at one another (and at us) do not lead us toward peace. How are these behaviors really avoiding the true problems in our culture? Journal about the ways in which you have added to this unproductive conflict addiction. In what ways has it become a way of life, not only in the dominant culture, but also in the church? How can you stop participating? How can the church better engage in productive conflict, the kind that leads to long-term peace?

Day 2:

    In either our culture or your personal life, identify a conflict through which a broader and deeper peace was achieved. Write a few words or sentences about the conflict and resolution. Stop and read what you have written. Take three deep breaths. Sit still and be present with God. Thank God for the peace that was achieved.

Day 3:

Most of us have conflicts we have been avoiding. Although there are times when this is effective, more often than not it escalates until the conflict becomes worse than it was originally. What conflicts are looming in your life? Write a few words or sentences about one specific conflict you may be avoiding. Stop and read what you have written. Take three deep breaths. Ask God to help you discern how to address this particular conflict. Sit still and listen for God. When you are ready, write three action steps you will take to move toward peace about this conflict.

Day 4:

There is no avoiding the violence in Deborah's story. Unfortunately, we don't seem capable of avoiding violence in our own stories either. Where do you see violence in your own life? Is it in the way someone speaks to you? the way you speak to another? What about the books, television shows, movies, or video games we consume? Where are the places that the "Prince of Peace" would want you to make changes?

Set a timer for three minutes. During that time, list the ways in which you are affected by violence. When you stop, take three deep breaths. Be still and listen for God. Ask God to lead you toward a more lasting peace.

Day 5:

Deborah called Barak to lead the necessary battle. Barak asked Deborah to be at his side. We all need help as we work through the conflicts in our lives. Identify your helper. Whom do you want by your side when you have to face conflict? Write a few words or sentences about this person to remind yourself how valuable he or she is. Reflect on those sentences. Thank God for this person. Write and mail a thank-you note to him or her.

Day 6:

God called Deborah to use her wisdom to lead the Israelites. God's call for prophets has not ended. Identify at least one area in which God is calling you to be a prophet. Write about your dreams, excitement, and fears about that call.

Day 7:

    Read Judges 4:4-9, 14-15. Now read it a second time, more slowly. Breathe deeply, and take in every word as you read the passage. Write down images, words, or phrases that jump out at you. Thank God for a good week. Rest in the peace that comes only from God.

The Wisdom Of Remembering

Scripture for lesson:
2 Chronicles 6:12-42

Written by Tiffany Hall McClung

FAITH
LIFE

When our son was very young, my husband and I felt consumed with the pressures of making our children into good human beings. It drove me crazy when our son would make a terrible choice like throwing a plastic truck at my head, not to mention the ensuing series of events.

First, a time-out would be declared. Like many young parents, we had a special chair that was used for time-out. I would march the toddler to the chair, say to him, at eye-level, "You are being put in time-out for throwing a truck at Mama's head. We don't throw things at people." Then I would set the timer, following the expert's advice, for one minute for each year of the child's life and walk away.

When the timer sounded, I would return to my child. Again at eye-level, I would ask, "Do you know why you were in time-out?" At least half of the time (or so it seemed), my son wouldn't have an answer. His lack of response made me certain he was a psychopath or that I was raising a serial killer.

Not four minutes earlier, I had clearly given him the answer. "You are in time-out for throwing a truck at Mama's head!" How was it possible that in four minutes this child had forgotten the reason? It made me crazy because there is wisdom in remembering why you are experiencing consequences. There is wisdom in remembering many things. There is wisdom in remembering our ancestors, wisdom in knowing that God remembers us, and there is wisdom in remembering God.

Prep for the Journey

Solomon is often connected with wisdom. By reminding the people of their covenant relationship with God, Solomon was giving them a way to remember God.

How has remembering brought wisdom to your life? When have you seen a failure to remember create a problem?

What promises have you made, only to find yourself straying from them? What were the consequences?

Cumberland Presbyterians often refer to themselves as "covenant people." What does that statement mean to you? What covenants have you made with others? How do contracts and covenants differ? Why does God covenant with us?

God made covenants with people beginning with Noah. God made a new covenant with Abraham and his descendants. These first covenants were promises from God and not dependent upon humans. However, this changed after God freed the people from slavery in Egypt. At this time the people had responsibilities within the covenant relationship, primarily to follow God's ways and leading. Despite having solemnly promised to keep the covenant, the people began to stray from their promises almost immediately.

First and Second Chronicles keep the idea of the covenant central as they record the vast history of the people of Israel, beginning with Adam and ending with the start of the Persian empire. That is a lot to cover in two books of the Bible (though some of it is covered in genealogies)! Although the chronicler covered a lot of history, the information has a definite slant. For instance, David and Solomon were presented as sterling examples of God's best, while the author conveniently left out many of their transgressions. Some scholars have even translated the titles of the books as "those things that were left out." They may have served as a "catchall" for what was not written in books like Samuel and the Kings (though there are overlapping stories in these books). While we do not know who wrote these books, the writing occurred between 400 and 500 B.C.E., which was several hundred years after the time of David and Solomon.

The Babylonian army overran Judah and took her people captive in the 6th Century B.C.E., which makes it easier to understand why remembering the covenant would have been so important to those who wrote these passages. The Israelites were not so far removed from the time of exile that they would have completely forgotten the consequences of breaking the covenant relationship. Remembering the covenant and being reminded that God keeps covenant with God's people would have been an encouraging word for people who lived in fear of returning to an oppressive state.

On the Road

Solomon, King of Israel, was responsible for having a "house for God" built. The events in this scripture took place after the Temple had been completed and was awaiting dedication.

Read 2 Chronicles 6:12-17.

Then Solomon stood before the altar of the LORD in the presence of the whole assembly of Israel, and spread out his hands. [13] ...Then he knelt on his knees in the presence of the whole assembly of Israel, and spread out his hands toward heaven. [14] He said, "O LORD, God of Israel, there is no God like you, in heaven or on earth, keeping covenant in steadfast love with your servants who walk before you with all their heart— [15] *you who have kept for your servant, my father David, what you promised to him. Indeed, you promised with your mouth and this day have fulfilled with your hand.* [16] *Therefore, O LORD, God of Israel, keep for your servant, my father David, that which you promised him, saying, 'There shall never fail you a successor before me to sit on the throne of Israel, if only your children keep to their way, to walk in my law as you have walked before me.'* [17] *Therefore, O LORD, God of Israel, let your word be confirmed, which you promised to your servant David.*

The writer's use of the phrase "whole assembly" meant that everyone was welcome and important. At the dedication of the Temple, Solomon forgot no one. From the moment Solomon began to address the people, we are called to remember that all are welcome and invited to enter into covenant with God.

Solomon called the people to remember God. Through his prayer, Solomon was inviting the people to listen and remember. It also reminded the people that God had made a promise to David, Solomon's father. That promise was being fulfilled with the dedication of the Temple. It is an important moment for the people not only to remember that God keeps God's promises, but to rededicate themselves, alongside the Temple, to keep promises to God and to one another.

Read 2 Chronicles 6:18-21.

"But will God indeed reside with mortals on earth? Even heaven and the highest heaven cannot contain you, how much less this house that I have built! [19] *Regard your servant's prayer and his plea, O LORD my God, heeding the cry and the prayer that your servant prays to you.* [20] *May your eyes be open day and night toward this house, the place where you promised to set your name, and may you heed the prayer that your servant prays toward this place.* [21] *And hear the plea of your servant and of your people Israel, when they pray toward this place; may you hear from heaven your dwelling place; hear and forgive.*

It is impossible to contain God—in a building or otherwise. For example, our language is totally insufficient for containing God. While we continue to argue over names for God, we would do well to remember this: Our imaginations can't even contain God. I have a pretty vast imagination, which makes this fact hard to believe sometimes. There is no amount of creativity, knowledge, Bible study, or even prayer that can reduce God to a human understanding.

Solomon had no misguided belief about containing God. While it seems he hoped the Temple would fulfill a promise of his ancestors and become a center for prayer and worship, he was not delusional about the ability to lock God into a box—not even into the Ark of the Covenant. The Temple would be a holy space; the ark would be kept sacred. Not even Solomon would enter the space in which it was kept. However, God would never be kept or hidden or tamed.

Which groups of people do we often fail to invite and welcome into the church?

To what promises do you need to rededicate yourself?

Why do you think there are so many disagreements about the names for God? How do you feel about using inclusive language when referring to God? Where in scripture do you find the names of God that include feminine as well as masculine images? Which name do you use when you pray privately?

What is the difference between a temple for God and a temple for God's name?

How do you define prayer? How do you pray? When are you most likely to pray?

Who are the oppressed in your community? How can you work for their freedom?

What does it mean to sin against God? How will you seek forgiveness and reconciliation?

The Temple was not a place to contain God, but a place through which God's name could be revealed to God's people. There is a difference between the Temple being a dwelling place for God and it being a place for God's name.

Scenic Route

In this section of the scripture we see the full structure of Solomon's prayer. Through seven petitions, Solomon left nothing to chance. The prayer served to remind Israel of the ways she had failed God in the past. It also served as a way to remind the people that God would never fails them and would continue to forgive again and again.

Read 2 Chronicles 6:22-23.

"If someone sins against another and is required to take an oath and comes and swears before your altar in this house, [23] may you hear from heaven, and act, and judge your servants, repaying the guilty by bringing their conduct on their own head, and vindicating those who are in the right by rewarding them in accordance with their righteousness."

Some scholars refer to the first petition as one regarding social justice. The prayer asks God to bring to justice those who have wronged others, which could be interpreted as setting those who are being oppressed free. This interpretation fits well with the history of Israel at the time Second Chronicles was written. Freedom from Babylonian captivity would still have been very much on the minds of Israelites. The first petition asks God to free the oppressed.

Read 2 Chronicles 6:24-25.

"When your people Israel, having sinned against you, are defeated before an enemy but turn again to you, confess your name, pray and plead with you in this house, [25] may you hear from heaven, and forgive the sin of your people Israel, and bring them again to the land that you gave to them and to their ancestors."

The second petition refers to sins against God rather than other humans. In other words, this petition is about breaking covenant with God. The prayer reminded those who had assembled that God's people had a history of breaking covenant and asked God always to forgive them when they returned for reconciliation.

Read 2 Chronicles 6:26-27.

"When heaven is shut up and there is no rain because they have sinned against you, and then they pray toward this place, confess your name, and turn from their sin, because you punish them, [27] may you *hear in heaven, forgive the sin of your servants, your people Israel, when you teach them the good way in which they should walk; and send down rain upon your land, which you have given to your people as an inheritance."*

Petition three continues along the lines of humans breaking covenant with God, but the consequences are now found in the natural world rather than in human enemies. Solomon petitioned God to send rain during a drought. The prayer called to memory the droughts that the Israelites had experienced in the past. It also reminded them that God had never failed to send rain, eventually.

Read 2 Chronicles 6:28-31.

"If there is famine in the land, if there is plague, blight, mildew, locust, or caterpillar; if their enemies besiege them in any of the settlements of the lands; whatever suffering, whatever sickness there is; [29] whatever prayer, whatever plea from any individual or from all your people Israel, all knowing their own suffering and their own sorrows so that they stretch out their hands toward this house; [30] may you hear from heaven, your dwelling place, forgive, and render to all whose heart you know, according to all their ways, for only you know the human heart. [31] Thus may they fear you and walk in your ways all the days that they live in the land that you gave to our ancestors."

Continuing in the theme of the natural world, the prayer then covered all other natural disasters along with other suffering or sickness. With its broad strokes, petition four reminded the people that God would be with them in and through everything.

Read 2 Chronicles 6:32-33.

"Likewise when foreigners, who are not of your people Israel, come from a distant land because of your great name, and your mighty hand, and your outstretched arm, when they come and pray toward this house, [33] may you hear from heaven your dwelling place, and do whatever the foreigners ask of you, in order that all the peoples of the earth may know your name and fear you, as do your people Israel, and that they may know that your name has been invoked on this house that I have built."

Petition five turned the prayer toward "foreigners." Solomon prayed for all people, not simply the Israelites. This petition reminds us of the vastness of God's love and calls us to remember that God's name is for all.

Read 2 Chronicles 6:34-35.

"If your people go out to battle against their enemies, by whatever way you shall send them, and they pray to you toward this city that you have chosen and the house that I have built for your name, [35] then hear from heaven their prayer and their plea, and maintain their cause."

Solomon lifted up those who might have to leave home to fight for their people in the sixth petition as he asked for protection in bat-

How do you feel about the concept of God punishing humanity through the natural world?

How can you help those who are dealing with natural disasters to experience God's presence?

Who are the foreigners in your midst? How can you help them to know that God's love is also available to them?

Regardless of your political views over current military involvement, those who are serving need your prayers and support. How will you let them know of your concern?

tle. In the all-inclusive nature of the entire prayer, Solomon reminded those listening that God would hear their prayers regardless of where they were when they prayed.

Read 2 Chronicles 6:36-39.

"If they sin against you—for there is no one who does not sin—and you are angry with them and give them to an enemy, so that they are carried away captive to a land far or near; [37] then if they come to their senses in the land to which they have been taken captive, and repent, and plead with you in the land of their captivity, saying, 'We have sinned, and have done wrong; we have acted wickedly'; [38] if they repent with all their heart and soul in the land of their captivity, to which they were taken captive, and pray toward their land, which you gave to their ancestors, the city that you have chosen, and the house that I have built for your name, [39] then hear from heaven your dwelling place their prayer and their pleas, maintain their cause and forgive your people who have sinned against you."

Finally, the writer addressed the fear of an exile for the Israelites. For those living during the time of the author of the Chronicles, the fear of exile was a very real and present worry. Once again, Solomon reminded the people of his day that they were sinful, that they were prone to breaking covenant with God, and that the Temple was no guarantee of trouble-free lives. However, the prayer served as a reminder that God's goodness and mercy would never fail.

Perhaps this prayer is one of the reasons Solomon is often connected with wisdom. Though it was likely written by someone else many years later, the writer placed these words in the mouth of this wise leader so that those listening and those reading it thousands of years later could witness the wisdom in remembering. Solomon forgot nothing and left out no one. In the dedication of the Temple, he took time to point to the truly important structure—that of the covenant life between God and God's people.

Workers Ahead — CAUTION

The prayer of Solomon ends with a reference to one of David's psalms, 132:8-10, known as "Song of Ascents." This reference is a beautiful literary way to close the prayer credited to David's own son, Solomon. It helps us to recall the ways in which the completion of the Temple was the fulfillment of promises made to David by God, and to God by David. There is a sense that we have come full circle and leave the prayer in the confidence that God always fulfills God's promises.

What reminds you that God's goodness and mercy will never fail?

When people say, "Prayer works," what do you think they mean? Think of other passages in the Bible that quote prayers. Who was doing the praying? What was the focus? How does your community pray together?

How have you experienced God's fulfillment of promises?

Read 2 Chronicles 6:40-42.

"Now, O my God, let your eyes be open and your ears attentive to prayer from this place.[41] *Now rise up, O LORD God, and go to your resting place, you and the ark of your might. Let your priests, O LORD God, be clothed with salvation, and let your faithful rejoice in your goodness.* [42] *O LORD God, do not reject your anointed one."*

Solomon's prayer mentioned those who are oppressed and foreigners. Using the discussion questions, your group would have identified people who are oppressed or foreigners. What type of actions did you identify that would be of benefit to these people? Take time now to plan how you will implement one or more of these actions.

Many congregations use their buildings for a myriad of activities from sports to worship to youth lock-ins to housing people who are homeless. Some people have trouble with the idea of using a facility built for worship for anything that is not specifically worship. However, many newer church facilities are built around a multi-purpose room that serves as a sanctuary, fellowship area, and many other things. Contrast the role of a house built for God's name in Solomon's time with churches of today. Talk about the positive and negative aspects.

In the Rear View

As a class, reflect on the ways in which God has fulfilled promises to your own faith community. Talk about the ways your church (Sunday school class or small group) has failed in promises made to God.

Review the seven petitions of Solomon's prayer. Consider which ones seem most important for your community right now. Why?

We often find ourselves in time-out without remembering how we got there. It seems that the prayer of Solomon is a guide to help us remember. It does a thorough job of pointing out what should be remembered. While the words of Solomon cover every possible scenario for the need of prayer, the bottom line is that God will always remember the covenant made with God's people. We would do well to do the same.

What forms of ministry is your faith community uniquely poised to offer because of the type of facility you have? How are you maximizing these opportunities?

The most obvious place we see promises made in our churches is when someone is baptized. What promises are made during that sacrament? by whom? How are you, as part of the community of faith, keeping those promises?

Travel Log

Day 1:

Grab a Bible and look for the different images, metaphors, and names used for God. A good place to begin is in the psalms. Or simply list from memory the many images you have heard used for God. Spend a few minutes reflecting on that list. Then journal a response to these questions: Which name or image for God holds the most power for you? Why?

Day 2:

Ask someone in your life—a family member, co-worker, or school mate—what images for God mean the most to him or her and why. Even if it is an image that makes you uncomfortable, listen and be present with the person you have asked. Thank the person for sharing. Find time today to write about that image and the person's experience with it. You may want to begin your writing with, "My (friend/co-worker/school mate) finds _____ to be the most powerful image for God in his or her life. As I listened to him or her speak about this, I found myself feeling…"

Day 3:

Solomon's prayer includes details that bring to mind every way humans fail God. The prayer is also a reminder to humans that God will never fail us. We believe that God wipes away and forgets our sins. Why, then, do you think it seemed important to Solomon to remember them? For what sins have you been forgiven, but you need not to forget? What is the value in remembering? Reflect on these questions during at least five minutes of quiet time. Listen for God in the silence. Journal about your experience following the time of quiet.

Day 4:

The scriptures for this lesson remind us again and again of God's faithfulness. At the core of that faithfulness is God's enormous capacity for forgiveness. We are created in God's image, and we are called to practice this same capacity for forgiveness. But we are not God, so it is hard.

Reflect on one or two people in your life who need your forgiveness. Write their names down in the space below. "Pray in color" as you doodle and make shapes around the names. You can use crayons, colored pencils, or markers. If you don't have these materials, simply doodle with whatever pen or pencil you have. See where your hand wants to take the pencil, and ask God to help you forgive as you have been forgiven.

Day 5:

There is wisdom in remembering. It is wise to remember our own sins in an effort to keep from repeating the same mistakes. The same is true for our history. Without boldly facing our history, we rarely move forward and are apt to repeat the mistakes of the past. It is also wise to remember all the goodness God has given us in our lives.

Today, take the time to remember the goodness. Journal about a loved one who has died and the wonderful memories you have of that person. Or write about your most peaceful, fun, or exciting memory. Memory is a gift and it is wise to use it.

Day 6:

What does it mean to you to you to be in covenant relationship with God? Write about the differences between covenant and contract. Spend time reflecting on the ways in which we continue to think of God as a contractual God rather than a covenantal God. Write a covenant between you and God. What are you willing to give God, and what are your expectations? After writing, read what you wrote and sit quietly as you listen for God's response.

Day 7:

Read through 2 Chronicles 6:12-42 again. Now read it a second time, more slowly. Breathe deeply, and take in every word as you read the passage. Write down images, words, or phrases that jump out at you. Thank God for a good week. Rest in the knowledge that God hears your prayers, never fails on a promise, and always forgives.

Speaking Words Of Wisdom

Scripture for lesson:
Proverbs

Written by Cardelia Howell-Diamond

What words of wisdom do you wish you had heeded? What words of wisdom do you think would be most helpful to younger generations? Why do people often resist hearing the wisdom in someone else's words?

Who might be considered a contemporary wisdom writer? Why?

Who helped you learn to manage everyday life?

The older I get, the smarter my parents get. Undoubtedly, many of us have had the same realization to some extent. I remember hearing my parents say things that I thought were so old fashioned, or even down right ridiculous. As I have grown and matured, I have come to understand that much of what my parents said was not only true, but were words of wisdom they were trying to hand down to me. However, sometimes I chose to ignore their words of wisdom.

Prep for the Journey

The Bible contains various types of literature: history, law, prophecy, poetry and songs, wisdom, Gospels, and letters. The wisdom books include Proverbs, Ecclesiastes, Job, and some of the psalms. Most ancient societies had wisdom literature, which may have influenced what we know as the Book of Proverbs.

It's rather ironic that Solomon is so closely associated with wisdom. Even though he purportedly asked for and received wisdom from God, he made some very unwise choices. He made treaties with many other kingdoms, allowed his 700 wives to worship the gods of their homelands, and even had altars built to these other gods.

Proverbs provides practical wisdom for everyday living and management of life. Although people tend to attribute all of the writings in Proverbs to Solomon, there are strong indicators that they were written by multiple authors over a span of as much as several hundred years.

The first ten chapters are written in a different form than later ones; they tend to be more instructional in nature, telling people what not to do and what will happen if they do. It's possible that these chapters were part of the education of young aristocrats. However, for the purposes of this lesson, we will refer to Solomon as the writer of the book.

Chapters 10:1–22:16 and 25:1–29:27 contain many of the proverbs with which most people are familiar. These sayings are often short and written in a way that gives them humor or sting, which makes them easier to remember. They may have originally been written as comparisons, but eventually any short sayings that contained a general popular truth also came to be called proverbs. These truths eventually became associated with the religion of Israel. Many scholars believe that Solomon actually did write these chapters as a way of passing down some of the wisdom he had received from God and from his life experiences.

Some of the more well-known proverbs are:
- "Gossips betray a confidence, but the trustworthy keep a secret" (Proverbs 11:14).
- "Pride goes before destruction, a haughty spirit before a fall" (Proverbs 16:18).
- "Charm is deceptive and beauty is fleeting; but a woman who fears the Lord is to be praised" (Proverbs 31:30).

There is very little about the Book of Proverbs that is similar to any other book of the Bible. It does not contain a plot line, nor does it have a set order. Rather it is a collection of attitudes and beliefs that would help to shape the conscience of those who read and followed the truths expressed.

On the Road

The Book of Proverbs begins with a description of its purpose. This is not a collection of sayings to be put in fortune cookies. It is the one book closest to a how-to manual found in scripture.

Read Proverbs 1:1-7.
The proverbs of Solomon son of David, king of Israel:
2 For learning about wisdom and instruction,
*   for understanding words of insight,*
3 for gaining instruction in wise dealing,
*   righteousness, justice, and equity;*
4 to teach shrewdness to the simple,
*   knowledge and prudence to the young—*
5 let the wise also hear and gain in learning,
*   and the discerning acquire skill,*
6 to understand a proverb and a figure,

What are some of your favorite proverbs?

What is unique about the Book of Proverbs to you? Why do you think it is valuable to the scriptures?

What does it mean to you to fear God? In what frame of mind do you enter God's presence?

What are some modern proverbs? What is the basis for them? How does their wisdom compare with that of the ones in the Bible?

the words of the wise and their riddles.
7 The fear of the LORD is the beginning of knowledge;
fools despise wisdom and instruction.

According to verse 7, wisdom begins when we fear God. Huh? In religious terms, especially in the Old Testament, *fear* is more closely aligned with awe or reverence. It is also a way the people of Israel expressed their loyalty and obedience to God.

Using proverbs was any easy way to teach people. These sayings were based on human experiences; some were taken from nature. By using things with which the people were already familiar, and using short phrases, they were easy for people to remember. This book was written to be applied to our daily lives.

Jesus may have considered the proverbs when he taught. His parables, although they were sometimes stories, also used familiar, everyday things and occurrences as a way of helping the people to grasp concepts.

Imagine sitting at the feet of the best teacher you've ever had or about whom you've heard. Every word that comes from this teacher's mouth is dripping with meaning, with practicality, with hope, with vision. That is what studying the Book of Proverbs can be like for each of us.

Read Proverbs 1:8-19.
Hear, my child, your father's instruction,
and do not reject your mother's teaching;
9 for they are a fair garland for your head,
and pendants for your neck.
10 My child, if sinners entice you,
do not consent.
11 If they say, "Come with us, let us lie in wait for blood;
let us wantonly ambush the innocent;
12 like Sheol let us swallow them alive
and whole, like those who go down to the Pit.
13 We shall find all kinds of costly things;
we shall fill our houses with booty.
14 Throw in your lot among us;
we will all have one purse"—
15 my child, do not walk in their way,
keep your foot from their paths;
16 for their feet run to evil,
and they hurry to shed blood.
17 For in vain is the net baited
while the bird is looking on;
18 yet they lie in wait—to kill themselves!
and set an ambush—for their own lives!
19 Such is the end of all who are greedy for gain;
it takes away the life of its possessors.

Listen to your elders; they have the knowledge that God wants you to have. No, those who are older do not always know what's right, but a person who has more life and faith experiences will likely have expertise that those who are younger will not possess. Be careful about who influences you. Not everyone has your best interests at heart. Some people are greedy for whatever they can gobble down. Watch out for people such as these.

Scenic Route

Solomon told the people to heed the advice of those who had proven themselves to be wise. This cry went out time and again in scripture. Listen to the words of the Lord, listen to the prophets, listen to Jesus. Solomon knew that telling others to listen wouldn't be enough to drive the point home, so he gave Wisdom the chance to speak.

Read Proverbs 1:20-25.

Wisdom cries out in the street;
in the squares she raises her voice.
21 At the busiest corner she cries out;
at the entrance of the city gates she speaks:
22 "How long, O simple ones, will you love being simple?
How long will scoffers delight in their scoffing
and fools hate knowledge?
23 Give heed to my reproof;
I will pour out my thoughts to you;
I will make my words known to you.
24 Because I have called and you refused,
have stretched out my hand and no one heeded,
25 and because you have ignored all my counsel
and would have none of my reproof.

The ancient Hebrews were fond of giving human characteristics to non-human things. The word for wisdom in Hebrew is feminine, so personifying wisdom as a woman was natural for Solomon. Wisdom doesn't seem to care much about the expected role of a woman in proper society. She smashed all of those stereotypes by drawing attention to herself, calling out in a loud voice, and speaking bluntly in the middle of the busiest sections of town.

In Wisdom's first-person tale, we get a glimpse of just how much God wants us to pay attention to the knowledge we are being offered. This knowledge is not for God's benefit, but for ours. Wisdom calls for the people to heed her words, to follow her counsel. She can no longer stand to watch the people suffer in foolishness and folly.

How can you determine which people have your best interests at heart?

From whom do you seek advice? Why? Who taught you words of wisdom? How have you passed on your knowledge to others?

When has someone offered you wisdom that you refused? What happened in the situation? What happened in your relationship?

When have you experienced God seeking you? Where do you see God seeking to offer wisdom today?

What keeps you from hearing God's wisdom?

Wisdom cried out to the people where they were—in the streets, at the entrance to the city—not in quiet corners where they were praying or studying. She sought the people so that they might hear her word and be saved. God, too, calls out to us wherever we might be and offers us knowledge. God is not content to wait for us to find or even to seek God on our own. Instead, God seeks us!

As this passage continues, we learn that Wisdom was crying out to prevent the people from experiencing a time when they would not be able to find her. Their hearts would have hardened; their actions would have made them unable to hear; and their foolishness would have kept them from seeing. Wisdom did not want this to happen, so she warned the people.

Read Proverbs 1:26-33.
I also will laugh at your calamity;
 I will mock when panic strikes you,
27 when panic strikes you like a storm,
 and your calamity comes like a whirlwind,
 when distress and anguish come upon you.
28 Then they will call upon me, but I will not answer;
 they will seek me diligently, but will not find me.
29 Because they hated knowledge
 and did not choose the fear of the Lord,
30 would have none of my counsel,
 and despised all my reproof,
31 therefore they shall eat the fruit of their way
 and be sated with their own devices.
32 For waywardness kills the simple,
 and the complacency of fools destroys them;
33 but those who listen to me will be secure
 and will live at ease, without dread of disaster."

Wisdom will laugh at their calamity. That doesn't sound like a loving, caring God to me. We must remember that this is poetry, and poetry uses many literary devices. The reference to laughing might be seen as poetic justice. The people would face the consequences of not listening to God's words and refusing to heed God's knowledge.

When have you missed out on a blessing because you ignored God's wisdom and advice? What would you do to help others avoid such a situation?

Does God ever give up on us? No. God always seeks to be in relationship with us and all people. What is being said here points more to the idea that our own stubbornness can keep us from experiencing God's love and knowledge, which leads us to disaster.

In the Rear View

As the children of God, we have a unique opportunity in this world. The things of the world are fleeting at best, and harmful at worst. The teachings of the Old and New Testaments help us as we struggle to live as God wants. We have the community of faith to strengthen and support us in times of need. We are blessed.

But we cannot keep those blessings to ourselves. We need to go out into our communities, offering God's wisdom to others. We need to acknowledge God's actions rather than take credit ourselves. We need to heed the warnings of Wisdom so that we might find security in God.

Make a list of those people in your community who need encouragement and wisdom. Find ways to reach out to them through interaction, prayer, notes, and relationship.

Travel Log

Day 1:

Read Proverbs 4. Write down two or three of the proverbs that stand out to you. What insights are familiar? Which are new? Which ones do you think you should share today? Record your responses below. Note some ways of sharing as well.

Day 2:

Read Proverbs 9. What do you think about the contrast of Wisdom and the foolish woman? How can you tell the difference? How can you be sure you are speaking words of wisdom to others? Journal about times when you have had to determine the difference between wisdom and foolishness.

Day 3:

Read Proverbs 10. These are some of the general sayings of Solomon. Which ones apply to your life right now? Why? Jot down some of the ones that are most meaningful to you at this particular point in your life.

Day 4:

Read Proverbs 13. What do you think about the sayings on wealth and poverty? How do they challenge you? Verse 18 says that those who ignore instruction will have poverty and disgrace. How do you reconcile that statement with the systemic poverty in our world? Record some of your musings, as well as some possible responses to poverty, in the space below.

Day 5:

Read Proverbs 16:16-19. Most of the people in the United States have a relatively affluent lifestyle, especially when compared to people in other parts of the world. How would you approach this passage with someone who is living in poverty? Create a list of at least five things that you will personally do to alleviate poverty.

Day 6:

Read Proverbs 31:10-31. People often use these verses as a description of the perfect wife. How do you react to these words? List those words or phrases in which you find comfort. Create a second list of the words or phrases that cause you discomfort. Journal about your lists.

Day 7:

   If you were to write your own book of proverbs, what would you include? Make a list of at least ten proverbs to share with your group at a later date.

'Tis the Season

Scripture for lesson:
Ecclesiastes 3:1-15

Written by Cardelia Howell-Diamond

About what seasons do you get excited? How well do you deal with the changing seasons of nature? How do you deal with the seasonal changes of your life?

Why would a book that is at odds with so much biblical teaching be considered a book of wisdom worthy of inclusion in Holy Scriptures?

Every morning my husband and I try to watch the local news together. My husband's favorite part of the newscast is the weather report, not because he cares so much about the weather, but because he cannot wait to see what new sayings the meteorologist has come up with that day.

Our meteorologist likes to create meters for the day. Some favorites are the muggy-meter, the fog-o-meter, and the mow-meter, which tells you if you can safely mow your lawn that day. My husband cannot wait for lawn-mowing season just so he can look out for this particular meter!

Just as we mow the lawn in the summer, we plant in the spring and harvest in the fall. There is a season for everything. There is wisdom in following these seasons. The same is true for the seasons of our lives.

Prep for the Journey

Ecclesiastes is one of the wisdom books of the Old Testament. The author seems to have been writing about the world as he saw it, or as he had experienced it. The book contains some excellent advice and truths. However, realizing that he couldn't affect the outcome of the seasons, he determined that the best thing one could do was to enjoy the daily pleasures of life—work, play, and family—while he or she had it. His outlook was not particularly uplifting.

The author of Ecclesiastes was focusing on human wisdom, not godly wisdom. His thoughts contrast sharply with the gospel message, and with much of the Old Testament. The rest of the Bible talks about relationships—with God and with others—as being of the utmost importance.

Ancient scholars had similar questions about the Book of Ecclesiastes. Some even saw it as heretical. However, after much controversy, it was accepted because the writer's pseudonym suggested that Solomon might have been the author. According to other sources, it was included in the biblical canon because it begins and ends with religious teachings. While the book continually addresses God, it seems to rely almost completely on human understanding or knowledge.

Ecclesiastes is similar to Proverbs. It does not tell a story or provide a factual account of importance to the people of God. Simply stated, it is a book of poetry, much like one might find in a journal or blog. These writings are those of a man who was struggling to find meaning in his life without leaning on anyone else's understanding or power. He was trying to make sense of the world around him.

On the Road

Viewing Ecclesiastes from the lens of poetry, instead of prophecy or history, allows us to experience the emotions and questions of the writer. This is a personal book, much like many of the psalms. The author was crying out, seeking the meaning of his life.

Read Ecclesiastes 3:1-8.
For everything there is a season, and a time for every matter under heaven:
² a time to be born, and a time to die;
a time to plant, and a time to pluck up what is planted;
³ a time to kill, and a time to heal;
a time to break down, and a time to build up;
⁴ a time to weep, and a time to laugh;
a time to mourn, and a time to dance;
⁵ a time to throw away stones, and a time to gather stones together;
a time to embrace, and a time to refrain from embracing;
⁶ a time to seek, and a time to lose;
a time to keep, and a time to throw away;
⁷ a time to tear, and a time to sew;
a time to keep silence, and a time to speak;
⁸ a time to love, and a time to hate;
a time for war, and a time for peace.

Life does have a certain cyclical nature to its passing. We all have witnessed the seasons of the earth passing from spring to summer to fall and to winter. We generally know what to expect during each of these seasons because we have been through them before. We also have stories, writings, and pictures from others who have lived through them. There are times when, even if we know what to expect, we can become overwhelmed with the season. In the midst of the

What is unique about the Book of Ecclesiastes to you? How do you feel about its inclusion in the Bible?

If someone were to look at your ponderings and questions about life, what wisdom might he or she gain? What truths could be learned from what you observe? from what you choose to omit?

Explore each set of seasons with a partner or as a group. What things come to mind? Which ones speak to you in your current context? Share responses as a total group.

How does the cyclical nature of life comfort you? frustrate you?

cloudy, gray days of winter, we may feel as if the sun will never shine again. In the dog days of summer, it seems that we will sweat ourselves into oblivion before it gets cool once more. In the icy grip of winter, we may feel as if we'll never experience warmth again.

Having observed the world around him, the author was trying to use its ordered sequence to help him find meaning for his life. Just as things happen again and again in the natural world, they do so in the lives of humans. The author listed things that were to be done and redone throughout one's life. (Scholars think that the reference to throwing and gathering stones was a metaphor for sexual intercourse within marriage.) While the list may seem very specific, it actually represents a broad spectrum of human activities.

God established all of the seasons in nature and in life. They come and go in an ordered manner, and humankind can do nothing to affect them. Realizing his helplessness must have been very frustrating and depressing for the writer. However, it would appear that he came to understand the wisdom in God's order.

Scenic Route

Reading through the list found in verses 1-8 might lead one to conclude that everything evens out in the end. In other words, why do anything if you're going to have to undo it? This kind of logic is much like the kind employed by many children when having to make their beds. "But Mom! Why do I have to make it if I'm just going to mess it up again tonight?" While there may be some validity to this line of thinking, the author of Ecclesiastes takes it one step farther.

Read Ecclesiastes 3: 9-11.

What gain have the workers from their toil? [10] I have seen the business that God has given to everyone to be busy with. [11] He has made everything suitable for its time; moreover he has put a sense of past and future into their minds, yet they cannot find out what God has done from the beginning to the end.

When have you felt like you were spinning your wheels? Does the concept of God handing out busy work resonate with you? What other analogies used here speak to you?

The author listed the events and their counterparts, but found that they added up to nothing. What was the point of it all? He went on to accuse God of handing out busy work to humanity. I'd say the author was having a rough time of things. This sounds like someone who was questioning who he was and why he existed. He was bored with the routine life seemed to have handed him. He felt as if he had no access to God's wisdom, so he painted a picture of a God who was more interested in keeping things moving than being in relationship with creation.

36

He also noted that God had not only given people a sense of the past, but of the future. That's a powerful statement. Even when things look dire, we have hope for a future—because God has given it to us. However, the author even found fault with that gift because God didn't also give people the ability to understand God's purposes or to "see the whole picture."

Workers Ahead

We cannot understand everything God has done or every reason God has for speaking or remaining silent. If we could, then we would be God—and we most assuredly are not! No matter how advanced we become, no matter how much we learn, we will not understand the Creator or creation apart from God's revelation.

Relying on his own understanding, the author appears to have felt as if God had set the planet spinning and didn't care what would happen next. Too often we fall into this same trap of self-sufficiency instead of relying upon God. It is tempting to feel that God has left us to fend for ourselves, especially in times of war, loss, grief, and pain.

Sometimes pain colors our view of God and God's work. We can become convinced that we know better, or that our way is the only way things should occur. The author, having found fault with God, proceeds to hand out his own advice for what is good and right in life.

Read Ecclesiastes 3:12-15.

I know that there is nothing better for them than to be happy and enjoy themselves as long as they live; 13 moreover, it is God's gift that all should eat and drink and take pleasure in all their toil. 14 I know that whatever God does endures forever; nothing can be added to it, nor anything taken from it; God has done this, so that all should stand in awe before him. 15 That which is, already has been; that which is to be, already is; and God seeks out what has gone by.

The author espoused an "eat, drink and be merry" philosophy. Enjoy the good life! He even went so far as to say that God has given you these good things to enjoy, so go for it! These words are hedonism in a nutshell. They are the same words for which advertisers across the world hope we will fall when encountering their marketing campaigns.

The more we have, the more we consume, the better we will feel. It sounds great, but it is a lie. There is nothing that can satisfy us other than being in relationship with God. God created us to be dependent upon God. Only God can make us whole. No matter what the world tells us, no matter what the writer of Ecclesiastes may have felt, nothing will quench our thirst like the living water, Jesus the Christ.

Why is it important for people to have a sense of the past as well as of the future?

When have you felt as if God had abandoned you? How did you process those feelings? What did you learn about yourself? What did you learn about God?

What is wrong with an "eat, drink, and be merry" philosophy? Recall a time when you fell for this ploy.

In the Rear View

Reflect about a time when you tried to fill the empty places in your life with things other than Christ. Share your thoughts with others, if you are comfortable doing so.

People around the world, in the next pew, next door, or in the next room are just like us; they are trying to find something to fill them. We all are looking for what will make us feel less lost, less alone, less depressed, less needy. My friends, it won't be found in self-help books or drug stores, success or monetary wealth. It doesn't come from relationships or from accolades or titles.

Only Jesus can bring us to a place of wholeness. Only Jesus can give us the satisfaction we seek. If you do not know him, learn about him. If you do know him, share him with others. Too many of us live our lives like the author of Ecclesiastes, convinced that we alone can give meaning to this life. Life without Christ is empty at best.

Travel Log

Day 1:

Write a journal or blog entry today that expresses how you feel about your relationship with God. Be open and honest; it is for your eyes only. You will build on this experience for the next few days.

Day 2:

Re-read your journal entry from yesterday. What things did you leave out? What opinions or experiences have changed? Edit as needed to reflect your relationship with God today.

Day 3:

Look at your journal entry again. This time, read it as if you are someone who does not know God. What would your words say about your faith? What might the reader learn about God through what you have said? What would you want them to learn that you might have left out? Edit and change as you feel led.

Day 4:

Write a response to your earlier journal entry. You could engage in a dialog with the entry or write a reflection on the process. Don't be overly critical of yourself, but be honest.

Day 5:

Write a letter to someone who is important to you who is struggling in his or her relationship with Christ or does not have a relationship with Christ. What do you want this person to hear? What experiences in your life might be helpful? How are you praying for this person? This initial letter is not to send, so feel free to write it in the space below.

Day 6:

Re-read, edit, and review your letter. Read it as the person receiving it might read it. What things are powerful? What could be left out? Where do you see God speaking to him or her through these words? Pray over this letter.

Day 7:

Read your letter once more. Have you ever received a communication similar to this from someone? If so, how did you respond? If you feel led, send the letter or email it once you have prayed and re-read it once more. Journal your feelings about this process.

Keeping It Simple

Scripture for lesson:
Micah 2:1-3; 6:6-8

Written by Tiffany Hall McClung

Many years ago, people started using the acronym KISS: Keep It Simple, Stupid (or Silly) as a way of reminding themselves and others that it's not necessary, or even helpful, to make things complicated. In fact, it seems that an entire industry has developed around this concept. There are now magazines, blogs, self-help books, closet organizers, cookbooks, meditation practices, and much more, all based on the idea of "simple living." I find it so fascinating that we have taken the idea of living simply and complicated it beyond all belief! But that seems to be what we human beings do. We take simple ideas or concepts, even faith, and then complicate them to the point that not one of us could keep up. Where is the wisdom in that?

Prep for the Journey

The prophet Micah is known as one of the minor prophets. However, he was anything but minor! Jeremiah (26:19) gives credit to Micah for a major repentance of the people that occurred during his time as a prophet. His writings include a lot of wisdom, especially in how we relate to one another and to God.

Micah's name means "Who is like Yahweh?" Scholars believe that Micah likely wrote the first part (chapters 1–3) of the book that bears his name. It is believed that chapters 4–7 were added at a later time and written by someone else.

Micah was from the small town of Moresheth, which was about twenty-five miles southwest of Jerusalem, along the border between Judah and the Philistine nation. However, Micah likely traveled to Jerusalem to deliver his prophecies. His sphere of influence would have been much larger in the city.

What simple concept have you made complicated? How can you simplify it again?

Who has helped you to understand how to relate to God? to one another?

How can we broaden our sphere of influence?

Where do you see the rich getting richer at the expense of those who are poor? What can you do to stop this oppression? What is the church's responsibility?

Where do people find hope today? How is the church offering hope?

Read Micah 2:1-3.

Alas for those who devise wickedness
and evil deeds on their beds!
When the morning dawns, they perform it,
because it is in their power.
² They covet fields, and seize them;
houses, and take them away;
they oppress householder and house,
people and their inheritance.
³ Therefore thus says the Lord:
Now, I am devising against this family an evil
from which you cannot remove your necks;
and you shall not walk haughtily,
for it will be an evil time.

Micah's prophecies condemned those with riches and power—not because they were rich and powerful, but for the way they used their wealth and power. They would lie awake at night, thinking of ways to get richer. Since wealth was closely tied to property ownership, they literally took fields and houses away from the owners. Such a loss caused many families to become slaves just in order to survive.

When the people moved into the Promised Land, God divided the land by tribe, with each tribe (except the Levites) receiving an appropriate share. The families in the tribes were then assigned certain portions, which was a sacred trust. Ownership of that land was supposed to remain with that family. If for some reason property had to be sold, it was to be returned in the Year of Jubilee. So, these rich land mongers were sinning against God and people.

Micah saw what was happening—the lack of moral fiber and the corruption—and refused to remain silent. Therefore, the message of the Book of Micah is one of hope for those who are the "least of these." Consequently, it is also a message of judgment for those who oppress them.

On the Road

Read Micah 6:6-8.

"With what shall I come before the LORD
and bow myself before God on high?
Shall I come before him with burnt offerings,
with calves a year old?
⁷ Will the LORD be pleased with thousands of rams,
with ten thousands of rivers of oil?

Shall I give my firstborn for my transgression,
    the fruit of my body for the sin of my soul?"
[8]*He has told you, O mortal, what is good;*
    and what does the LORD require of you
but to do justice, and to love kindness,
    and to walk humbly with your God?

The above verses comprise the most recognized passage of Micah, and would likely make a list of most quoted biblical passages. In fact, when Jimmy Carter was inaugurated in January of 1977, the Bible upon which he rested his hand to take the oath of office was opened to these verses. There is something, especially in verse 8, that appeals to us as God's people. It is the simplicity of the faith.

The simple idea of loving God and loving neighbor has been around for thousands of years, influencing Isaiah and Micah, as well as Jesus. And yet, we humans continue to complicate things! Verses 6-7 comment about the absurdity of trying to complicate this simple idea.

Beginning with burnt offerings (meaning the entire animal would have been used, nothing remaining for a meal) and progressing to a year old calf, thousands of rams, rivers of oil, and finally the firstborn of the transgressor is a rhetorical device leading to the answer in an effort to point out the absurdity of it all. There was no way the people who were being oppressed would have had the resources to sacrifice even one animal without keeping some for food, much less rivers of oil! These examples called to mind the affluence of their oppressors.

We are comfortable in the complicated, for some reason. We prefer ten detailed commandments over the two in which Jesus summarized them. We ask God for a list of sacrifices that will make God happy, but refuse to believe God when we are told none of that is required.

The answer from God is as simple as it gets. "What does God require of you?" The answer is simple: "Just you!" That's it. God wants you, not your belongings or sacrifices, just you. There is no thing that God requires. This scares us to death, which leads us to complicate matters, not only in our own lives, but also in the lives of those around us.

Scenic Route

Scholars believe that what we know as the Book of Micah was a worship resource for the community. These exchanges between God and God's people would have played out in public worship as a reminder to the people of the hope that is ever-present. Worship would have been a time that was a safe for the people to reveal the pain and

Where do you find wisdom in Micah's teachings? How can you apply that wisdom in your life?

Cumberland Presbyterians are not bringing burnt sacrifices to church on Sunday (I'm assuming!) but, we do make sacrifices in an effort to please God. What do those sacrifices look like in your own life? in the life of your faith community? We know that God doesn't require sacrifices, so why do our actions often not support what we claim to believe?

Sometimes being completely honest in worship is scary and difficult. In what ways do you find it safe to address your own doubts, fears, questions, and anger in worship? How does your liturgy (calls to worship, hymns, prayers of confession, creeds, etc.) address the real needs you have to be honest in worship?

"Be the best you that you can be" sounds like a bumper sticker! When we put it into the context of Micah 6:8, how does it change from a self-help slogan to a simplified, but dynamic, faith? In what ways could your life be different in an effort to live this way? In what ways do you do justice, love kindness, and walk humbly with the Lord?

How do you reconcile the seeming difference between God not requiring anything of you, but then saying that you should "do justice"? What do you hope to gain by "doing justice"?

In what ways have you been made to feel like you weren't good enough for God's love?

suffering they were experiencing at the hands of the rich and powerful. They would have been invited to "act out," through the liturgy, the dynamic nature of the relationship with God. Perhaps this is why we have four chapters in addition to those that are believed to be Micah's words. Try to imagine these later chapters as having grown out of a vibrant worshiping community that was attempting to address its fears, as well as hopes, in an authentic way.

Read Micah 6:8 again.
He has told you, O mortal, what is good;
and what does the LORD require of you
but to do justice, and to love kindness,
and to walk humbly with your God?

As if understanding that God's children like to complicate things, Micah 6:8 attempts to keep it simple while providing a little more guidance than simply, "All God wants is YOU!" While that is absolutely true, God provides us a formula to use for simplicity. Micah may have been the original *Living Simple* magazine!

It's as if God were saying, "Just be yourself. Do justice. Love Kindness. Walk humbly with me." Micah simplified the teachings of other prophets. Doing justice is the primary theme in Amos; loving kindness is from Hosea; and walking humbly points us toward the call of Jesus in the New Testament. The Book of Micah deals with justice, peace, and the Messiah. It is a call to hope.

Workers Ahead   CAUTION

It gets confusing when we are told that nothing is required of us, but then hear that we should "do justice." Justice is not simply an ideal; it requires us to take action, to work for justice. While this may appear to indicate that we can "earn our way into heaven through good works," that is not the case. When our relationship with God is active and dynamic, it will lead us to action.

The people of Micah's world had been oppressed to the point that they felt as if they had nothing to offer God. When they looked at the sacrifices and offerings the wealthy could bring, they felt even more downtrodden.

We live in a world that is constantly telling us that we are not good enough. According to the world, we need this car or that house or this energy drink or that diet plan or this new gadget or that dating site, etc. Once you have these things, then you might be good enough. We serve a God who quietly whispers, "You are mine, my beloved. You are enough." It often becomes too difficult to hear those whispers over the screams of the world.

Micah's words were not meant to add complexity to the people's faith, but to help them believe that they were good enough simply because they were God's children. The same applies to us. Keep it simple. There is wisdom in that.

As a group, discuss the ways in which you can each "do justice, love kindness, and walk humbly with God" in the coming weeks. What comes naturally to you? What are you already doing? In what ways do you want to simplify? In what ways could you possibly do more? Share your goals with the group. When you are together again, be prepared to update one another.

In the Rear View

The Book of Micah gave hope to the hopeless. It is a reminder that God is with the most rejected and oppressed of all people. It is a celebration that God loves us and requires nothing but ourselves.

Speak boldly and honestly with one another about your own expectations of followers of Christ. God says that nothing is required but to be ourselves. In what ways has the church in general, and your own faith community in particular, communicated the opposite to others? Is there a dress code for worship? Are addicts welcome? What about the homeless? people of another ethnicity?

Dream together about what worship could look like if these ideas were included in the liturgy. How are God's children made to feel that they are simply enough in worship? If time permits, write a prayer or a litany together to use in worship. Give it to the pastor or worship team and ask that it be used when appropriate.

What will help you to remember the wisdom of keeping your faith simple?

How do your expectations of followers of Christ interfere with your ability to share your faith?

Travel Log

Day 1:

Find a quiet place where you will not be interrupted as you pray. Your prayer is this: "Thank you, God. I am enough." For five minutes, breathe deeply and repeat this phrase in your mind. Journal about this experience when you are done.

Day 2:

We believe the world's lies about ourselves. We also allow those lies lead us to believe that others are not good enough. Where are you most judgmental about God's children? They are the ones for whom you are praying today. Again, find a quiet place where you can pray without interruption. Your prayer today is this: "Thank you, God. They are enough." Insert specific names or even titles of groups of people for "they." Repeat this phrase as you pray. Journal about this experience when you are done.

Day 3:

What areas of your life could be simple, but you have found ways to complicate them? List and reflect on those areas. Ask God to help you simplify your life so that you can be the best you that you can be. Following a time of prayer, make a short list of action steps that will enable you to simplify these things. Follow through

with your action steps.

Day 4:

Read Micah 6:8. Think of the ways in which you have heard it quoted and used throughout the years. Why do you think it is such a popular scripture? Include the reasons it is important to you as well. Record your thoughts.

Day 5:

Find a bulletin from your church, and look through the liturgy. (If your church doesn't use printed bulletins, make a list of the worship order used each week.) Journal about the ways in which worship helps all people to feel loved, accepted, and valued. How are children included in worship? older people? If you feel there

are issues that need to be addressed, take them to your pastor or worship team.

Day 6:

Find a way to live authentically into your faith. "Do justice" today. How that looks will depend on you. Share some thoughts about your experience when you are done. Write honestly about the ways in which you still attempt to please God with your "doing." Return to the prayer from Day 1: "Thank you, God. I am enough."

Day 7:

Read Micah 6:6-8. Now read it a second time, more slowly. Breathe deeply, and take in every word as you read the passage. Write down images, words, or phrases that jump out at you. Thank God for a good week. Rest in the knowledge that God finds you to be absolutely enough!

The Boy Jesus

Scripture for lesson:
Luke 2:39-52

Written by Tiffany Hall McClung

When my children were toddlers and preschoolers, it seemed they were constantly asking questions. "Why is the sky blue?" "How does an acorn grow into a tree?" "Where do babies come from?" It's a cliché used in books and movies all the time, but that's what it felt like many times.

While I had moments of frustration when I would simply say, "No more questions right now!" for the most part I loved it. I loved it because I could see the brain of my own child growing through those questions. I knew that he or she was learning by asking those things, things that sometimes had no answer.

What was even more fascinating to me was the way in which I grew through those questions. While at first I might have believed I had a perfect answer, there would be a follow-up question that would throw me for a loop. It would send my own mind meandering down the lane of exploration and deeper thought. My children taught me what I really thought and believed by asking me questions. My hope is that I learned something from them and that I ask more questions than I answer.

Prep for the Journey

The Gospel of Luke is the only account of the life of Jesus that includes a story of him as a boy. Mary and Joseph fulfilled the Jewish laws regarding their infant son—circumcising, naming, presenting him at the Temple, and offering the sacrifice of two small birds. Once the story revealed that Mary and Joseph were model Jewish citizens, time passed in the book. The writer of Luke used verse 40 to show this passage of time. Luke resumed his account when Jesus was twelve years old.

How have questions helped you to grow, especially in your faith? How can you help others to grow by asking questions?

Why do you think Luke was the only Gospel writer to include this story?

Read Luke 2:39-43.

When they had finished everything required by the law of the Lord, they returned to Galilee, to their own town of Nazareth. ⁴⁰ The child grew and became strong, filled with wisdom; and the favor of God was upon him. ⁴¹ Now every year his parents went to Jerusalem for the festival of the Passover. ⁴² And when he was twelve years old, they went up as usual for the festival. ⁴³ When the festival was ended and they started to return, the boy Jesus stayed behind in Jerusalem, but his parents did not know it.

In Jewish custom, all adult males were to travel to Jerusalem for three annual festivals—Passover, Pentecost, and Tabernacles (Exodus 23:1-17; 34:22-23; Deuteronomy 16:16). Because of the distance for some residents, Passover was the only mandatory journey. It was also customary that around the age of twelve or thirteen, a boy would become a "son of the commandment," which would have been similar to what many of our churches do in confirmation. In Jesus' culture, it would have been a sign that he was an adult. It is possible that Jesus was traveling to Jerusalem for Passover in preparation for the transition from boy to man.

It is interesting that Mary made the pilgrimage as well. Women were not required to do so. Mary's presence among those traveling was a sign of her devotion to her faith and her family. This journey of about 80 miles would have taken approximately three days.

In writing about this story, Fred Craddock points to some interesting facts regarding its structure. For example, the literary model used by the writer of Luke seems to be taken from 1 Samuel 2 and 3 with the dedication of Samuel at the temple, Samuel's return to the temple as a young boy, and his call, which he experienced in the temple. Sometimes Luke even used the same phrasing as found in 1 Samuel 2 and 3. The Gospel of Luke often does this sort of thing deliberately, making connections to the Hebrew Scriptures that the readers/listeners would have understood. For Luke, this was an ever-important reminder that the Hebrew Scriptures of their faith and history were intricately connected to the story of Jesus.

On the Road

Read Luke 2:44-47.

Assuming that he was in the group of travelers, they went a day's journey. Then they started to look for him among their relatives and friends. ⁴⁵ When they did not find him, they returned to Jerusalem to search for him. ⁴⁶ After three days they found him in the temple, sitting among the teachers, listening to them and asking them questions. ⁴⁷ And all who heard him were amazed at his understanding and his answers.

What customs have been important in your faith journey? Why?

What significance has this particular story held in your life? How has it shaped the way you read the other Gospels? How much attention have you paid to it?

In what situations would you feel comfortable assuming a child for whom you were responsible was part of the group? Why?

How does it make you feel to know that Jesus pushed the boundaries in much the same was as young people continue to do?

When have you found yourself amazed at the wisdom of a child? How likely are you to listen to a child's thoughts? How seriously does your faith community respond to the needs and ideas of its children?

We may wonder how parents could not have known the whereabouts of their own son. Mary and Joseph assumed "he was in the group of travelers." The people would have traveled in groups for safety, and to enjoy the companionship of others. There would have been enough people in the caravan for Mary and Joseph each to feel sure that Jesus was with his friends, the other parent, or another family. Imagine families in church feeling secure, knowing that their children are running around "somewhere" in the building with trusted friends."

As a twelve-year-old, Jesus was also likely pushing the boundaries between childhood and adulthood, seeking more independence. At the end of their first day of the return trip, everyone likely came together for a meal or to find places to sleep. At that point Jesus' parents realized he was not among the travelers. Presuming they were a day's journey out, Mary and Joseph began the trip back, probably retracing their steps and searching along the way. After three days, his parents located him sitting among teachers in the Temple.

The scripture also tells us that Jesus was "listening to them [teachers] and asking them questions." The asking of questions was an ancient rabbinical method of teaching. That Jesus was asking questions is a clue that Jesus was not simply receiving information, but that he was also actively engaged in teaching. It is clear that those listening to the boy Jesus saw wisdom in him. They were "amazed" as they listened to this boy, not yet a man, reflect on the faith in ways that opened their own eyes to new understandings.

For the Gospel of Luke, it was important that the narrative of Jesus' birth and childhood begin and end in the Temple. The infant was dedicated in the Temple as was required, and the boy Jesus taught and learned in the Temple—an indication of the life he would lead. There is a school of thought that attempts to strip away the Jewish faith from the teachings of Jesus. For Luke, this was impossible. Any distance between Jesus and the Temple was not a sign of God's rejection of the Jewish faith or people. Instead it was a sign of the people's (and religious leaders') rejection of Jesus. In the Gospel of Luke, Jesus was intimately connected to the Temple, and therefore, to his Jewish faith.

Scenic Route

Read Luke 2:48-49.

When his parents saw him they were astonished; and his mother said to him, "Child, why have you treated us like this? Look, your father and I have been searching for you in great anxiety." [49] *He said to them, "Why were you searching for me? Did you not know that I must be in my Father's house?"*

Mary made it clear that she did not view Jesus as an adult. "Child," she called to him, as if to remind him of his place in the family. She reprimanded him and expressed her frustration, fear, and anger, just as any mother who had been looking for her child for three days would do. It is always good to see these perfectly human responses from "the holy family." It makes the fights over homework and green beans in my house a little more bearable!

Then Jesus spoke. These are the first recorded words of Jesus in the New Testament. If I had been Jesus' mother, I think his response would have just made me angrier. "Why were you searching for me? Did you not know that I must be in my Father's house?" Some very important things were happening in those two short questions.

First, it is important to note that Jesus answered the question with questions. He continued to follow the teaching discourse as a way of helping his own parents grasp God's call on his life. This call would not only affect Jesus, but all those who loved this boy. Through the questions, Jesus caused his parents to dig deeper into their own faith.

Second, scholars say that Jesus' reply was the first of many "it is necessary" statements found in the Gospel of Luke. Our translation says, "that I must be," but another way of translating this section is "it is necessary that I be about my Father's work." In Luke's Gospel, the Temple would continue to be a place where Jesus taught God's ways. Therefore, we can conclude that the boy Jesus was foreshadowing his public ministry as a rabbi, which was to come. The Temple and God's teachings/ways are intricately connected for Jesus in Luke's Gospel.

Third, Jesus' use of the personal pronoun should not go unnoticed. He was talking about an intimate relationship with God. In the customs of the time, Jewish people would have talked about God in a communal sense. If Jesus had been following custom, he would have said, "Did you not know that I must be in our Father's house?" Even more likely, he would have added the phrase "in heaven," so that he would have called God "our Father in heaven," in the same way he did when teaching the disciples how to pray. These may seem like small differences, but the point is significant. Even as a child, Jesus was so connected to God that he was bold enough to refer to God as "my Father." He was teaching a new way of viewing God by implying that God is not "in heaven," but in the here and now.

Workers Ahead

Read Luke 2:50-52.

But they did not understand what he said to them. ⁵¹ Then he went down with them and came to Nazareth, and was obedient to them. His

---

What might you have said to Jesus? How would you have felt about his response?

What do you think Mary and Joseph learned from this experience? What was Jesus trying to teach them?

Jesus taught his disciples to pray as a community, "Our Father...." He also taught that being part of a community was of great importance. However, today people often think of their relationship with God as so personal that they bypass the community. How do we damage the community by making our faith personal and private?

In what ways do questions play an important role in our community of faith and its worship? What makes worship in your faith community a safe place to ask had questions? What are you seeking in worship?

Which children in your congregation teach through questions? How do we honor these children? How do we celebrate the ways in which they are teaching us?

How is the growth of your faith connected to that of the community in which you worship and learn? Talk about specific ways you have seen these connections. In what specific ways you have aided the growth of others?

mother treasured all these things in her heart. [52] *And Jesus increased in wisdom and in years, and in divine and human favor.*

Jesus used questions to teach his own parents about his identity. Although they did not understand, Mary "treasured all these things in her heart." A better way of expressing that sentiment might be, "Mary pondered Jesus' questions and dug deeper into her own faith." We know that Jesus increased in wisdom, but what about the wisdom of Mary and Joseph?

Pondering our faith is an important part of our growth in wisdom. At the foundation of that growth is the study of scripture, worship, and prayer in community. Jesus seems to have been flabbergasted that his parents did not look for him in the Temple first. The work he had to do to be prepared for his ministry was work to be done in the Temple among the community. It was work that required prayer. It was work that required study of the scriptures. It was work that required asking hard questions and listening to the responses of other teachers.

We have all met young children who ask questions, wise questions, which seem beyond their years. We sometimes call such children "old souls." A question is asked that causes the adult being asked to dig deeper into his or her own faith. There are rarely answers. The next time such a situation occurs, remember Jesus in the Temple!

In the Rear View

Take a walk together as a class—preferably outside. Use this time to move your bodies differently than just sitting in a classroom. You may be surprised by what new insights you gain from prayer walking.

As you walk, reflect together about how you seek growth in wisdom. How often do you sit silently together? How willing are you to ask hard questions of one another? How do you allow every voice in the community to be heard? How could you be better at these practices? Is this time together merely an intellectual exercise, or are you digging deeper into your own faith and in so doing, assisting others in the community to do the same? This process is an ancient form of prayer—prayer walking or walking a labyrinth.

If you have time, work together to write a covenant for the ways in which you will practice faith in community in a way that leads to growth for all.

Travel Log

Day 1:

Write down everything you can remember about the call of Samuel. After you have done this, read 1 Samuel 2 and 3. What had you forgotten about Samuel's story? What similarities do you see between the scripture for this lesson and the one from the Old Testament? Journal for a few minutes on these two stories and what they mean in your own faith journey.

Day 2:

The writer of Luke intentionally connected Jesus to the Temple. Knowing that Jesus was a Jewish rabbi who understood his own faith well, why might it be important to know more about Judaism? How might studying Jewish teachings help you to connect to the life of Christ more fully? After two minutes, write down the first things that come to mind. Explore your own faith and the ways it relates to the Temple (the representation of Jesus' faith).

Day 3:

There is often much discussion about why this story is the only one in the Bible of Jesus between infancy and adulthood. Might the reason be that going through puberty was as hard for Jesus as it is for us?

Find pictures in some old magazines, and use them to create a collage that reminds you of the feelings of adolescence. If you prefer, draw, doodle, or color rather than make a collage. As you reflect on your own adolescence, imagine Jesus at this age. In what ways do you feel more connected to him through this exercise? Journal about your experience.

Day 4:

Questions were an important part of Jewish teaching, but we live in a society that wants answers. Reflect on your own need for definitive answers juxtaposed against Jesus continuing to ask questions. What does this tell you? Why are questions important? What questions do you have about your own faith?

Imagine you are with Jesus at the Temple. What questions is he asking you? How is he teaching you? Record your responses. Spend time considering those questions, knowing that it is okay not to have answers right now.

Day 5:

Put yourself in the place of either Mary or Joseph as they searched for Jesus. Think of the people they would have encountered. Consider the dangers to which they were exposed by traveling back to Jerusalem at night and alone, and by returning to Nazareth without the protection of the group. Choose one or more of these scenarios, and write a journal entry from the perspective of Mary or Joseph.

Day 6:

Slowly read the two questions in verse 49. Use the space below to record the significance of these words to you. Read over what you wrote. Reflect on what the Holy Spirit is teaching you through this time.

Day 7:

Read through Luke 2:39-52. Now read it a second time, more slowly. Write down images, words, or phrases that jump out at you. Remember that while the journey with Jesus is full of questions, those questions lead to a deeper faith.

Boiling It Down

Scripture for lesson:
Matthew 5:1-12

Written by Tiffany Hall McClung

FAITH
L
I
F
E

Boiling something down means stripping an ingredient down to its essence, removing anything that is extra and unnecessary. Boiling it down gets at the heart and importance of the item.

My husband's family owned a BBQ restaurant for seventy-five years. When I met my husband, he worked daily at the family business. He had the distinct smell not only of barbecued pork, but of what was probably the most unique part of the business: the Ollie's BBQ sauce. That sauce is still available in grocery stores, but it isn't the same. Just ask my husband! The difference is in the cooking.

For over seventy years, the recipe was passed from father to son to grandson to great-grandson. The sauce was slow-cooked in an enormous vat. When the restaurant closed its doors in 2001, my husband wanted to put the vat in our basement so he could continue to make the sauce! The sauce was so special because it was boiled down to its essence, leaving only the best of each ingredient. When mixed together, the end result was the best of the best. It isn't the complexity of the ingredients or the recipe. The secret is boiling it down.

Prep for the Journey

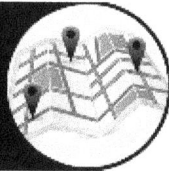

Our scripture comes from the passage known as "The Sermon on the Mount." The Gospel writer gives us clues as to the importance of this moment in Jesus' ministry. This sermon was the first major event following the baptism and temptation of Jesus and his call of the disciples. Further evidence of its importance is the location. Delivering this sermon from a mountain calls to mind Moses and his delivery of the Ten Commandments from Mt. Sinai. This connection to the Old Testament Law was important; by boiling down the Law to its essence, Jesus was teaching that the Law was not to be discarded. Rather, followers of the Law needed to seek after the Law's spirit.

> Think of the ways you can boil down your faith to its very essence. How would you teach others to boil down their faith?

> What signals the significance of an event to you?

Jesus was not teaching something new in this sermon, but was properly interpreting the Torah to his disciples. Where others had complicated the Law of God, Jesus wanted to boil it down to what was truly important, the heart of the matter. There was wisdom in his approach.

Read Matthew 5:1-2.

When Jesus saw the crowds, he went up the mountain; and after he sat down, his disciples came to him. ² Then he began to speak, and taught them.

The writer of Matthew was not only asking the reader to understand the importance of the moment, but also the importance of Jesus as Messiah. We see this messianic emphasis in phrases like "he sat down," which would lead a listener of the time to understand that Jesus was the teacher and the center of what was transpiring on that mountain. "His disciples came to him" reinforces this line of thinking; they were like royal subjects appearing before the king. In addition to the phrasing used in the text, these verses would have called to mind Isaiah 61:1-4. The Isaiah passage is an antecedent to the Matthew passage. For Matthew, the sermon not only provided a distilled understanding of what it meant to be a disciple, but it also magnifies our understanding that Jesus is the Messiah.

On the Road

The majority of people in our time associate the word *beatitude* specifically with Jesus and his teachings in the "Sermon on the Mount." However, the beatitude was a common Jewish literary form, which can be found throughout the Hebrew scriptures as well as in extra-biblical sources. But the ways in which Jesus' beatitudes led the least of these to find comfort, hope, and eternal life were not common. Jesus' beatitudes provided a specific outcome along with the blessing. He systematically arranged his teaching in a way that was not found in the Hebrew scriptures. Once again, Jesus took his own faith and knowledge of the Torah and reshaped it to deepen his disciples' understanding of their faith. In this way, he fulfilled rather than destroyed what God had begun through Moses. Jesus showed wisdom by indicating that he was the fulfillment of the Law of Moses.

Read Matthew 5:3-10.

"Blessed are the poor in spirit, for theirs is the kingdom of heaven.
⁴ "Blessed are those who mourn, for they will be comforted.
⁵ "Blessed are the meek, for they will inherit the earth.

How do you communicate what you believe about the Christ? How easy or difficult is it for you to do so?

How does your knowledge of the Old Testament affect your faith?

How do the beatitudes indicate a fulfillment of the Law?

⁶ "Blessed are those who hunger and thirst for righteousness, for they will be filled.
⁷ "Blessed are the merciful, for they will receive mercy.
⁸ "Blessed are the pure in heart, for they will see God.
⁹ "Blessed are the peacemakers, for they will be called children of God.
¹⁰ "Blessed are those who are persecuted for righteousness' sake, for theirs is the kingdom of heaven.

The first eight beatitudes mark a closed paragraph, rhetorically speaking. The first and eighth statements both end with "for theirs is the kingdom of heaven." That statement separates this passage from the next section, which is markedly different.

In Matthew's Gospel, Jesus' references to the "kingdom of heaven" indicate two things. First, a doctrinal idea points the listener to the eternal nature of life with Christ. Second, and not less so, is the present moment where God's kingdom breaks into our lives in the here and now. In other words, Jesus was not simply saying to his disciples, "Hey, I know it is hard and things look rough, but hold on through this life because there will be pie in the sky once it is over." For Jesus, the coming of the kingdom had already begun. Boiling down the Law into these statements was part of proclaiming that fact and aiding people in living it out in their (and our) daily lives.

To separate the beatitudes from the dynamic kingdom of God, making them into personal and autonomous statements for individual living is to strip them of their true power. While I loved listening to Robert Schuller with my mother on Sunday mornings while we got ready for our own church, reducing the beatitudes into pithy self-help quotes—the Be "Happy" Attitudes—is to remove them from the significance Matthew wanted us to understand in Jesus' most prominent sermon.

While distilling the Law into its most important form, Jesus also preached about an inclusiveness that may have been shocking to most of the followers. Through the first eight statements, Jesus left no stone unturned. Those in the society of the time who would have been locked out and kept away from places of worship, businesses, and family would have been hungry to hear this sermon. Jesus included them all—the poor, the meek, the peacemakers, etc. While these statements boil down faith for us, the sermon is also a testimony to the fact that Jesus called the least of these to be his disciples and assured them that God would bless them.

In regard to the wording itself, some scholars argue that translating the original documents into English has caused some problems. Most common translations today will use the words *happy* or *blessed*. The latter is often chosen because of the religious connotations it has for our society. Others believe a better translation would be *congratulations*. Because of the connection to the Jewish custom of using these kinds of statements, the most common belief is that the closest we can get in English to the idea of the beatitudes is *how fortunate are*. Regardless of the translation, the meaning leads us to an ethic for

When do you remember first hearing the beatitudes? How have they been meaningful in your life?

What stands out when first reading the beatitudes? What do you notice that you never have before?

Who is included in the first eight beatitudes? Who is left out? Where do you see yourself in these statements?

Many congregations struggle to get members involved in the work of the church. How might helping people understand the difference between disciples and believers address this issue?

When have you felt persecuted because you expressed your faith? How did you react? How have you changed as a result?

How do you define a prophet? Why does it seem prophets are always persecuted? What about our society makes being a prophet difficult? Why might it be easier to be a prophet somewhere else? What can your faith community do to make it easier for prophets to exist without persecution?

living as a disciple of Christ. It is both a call to action and a promise from God.

Many people prefer to call themselves "disciples" rather than "believers." There is an intentionality in this. Jesus has disciples, not believers, because more is expected than a mental exercise of faith. Our beliefs should be actualized in behaviors. This sermon of Jesus gives us the essential parameters for doing so.

Scenic Route

Read Matthew 5:11-12.

"Blessed are you when people revile you and persecute you and utter all kinds of evil against you falsely on my account. [12] Rejoice and be glad, for your reward is great in heaven, for in the same way they persecuted the prophets who were before you.

This section of the scripture passage is clearly different than the first eight beatitudes. There is a shift in voice. Suddenly, we have "blessed are you" rather than "blessed are they." It becomes more personal and targeted. It is worth exploring why, but it is also unlikely that we will know the true reason. Some scholars believe that it was commentary added by the writer to what was original. The parallel account in Luke 6:20-23 uses this rhetorical device throughout. Perhaps the writers were working from similar source material. Whatever the reason for the change in voice, the last two verses bring things up close and personal. Perhaps we could hear Jesus speaking directly to us in the eight previous points, or perhaps we envision others through his teachings. At this point Christ may be addressing each of us individually, or he may be speaking to the collective group of disciples.

In this conclusion to the beatitudes, Jesus said that living as one of his disciples wouldn't be easy. His words call to our minds the persecution of prophets from the beginning of time. Prophets have always been persecuted! Yet he invited us to rejoice because living in the kingdom of God is worth it.

Again, for Matthew, this kingdom was not some other-worldly place for which we are waiting. In light of these two verses, the kingdom is a lifestyle that we are invited to live right here and right now. We, as disciples, usher in the kingdom of God on earth.

Jesus preached a good sermon. He gave us eight identifiable points through which he made clear that God's ways are different from our ways. In the final section of the scripture passage, Jesus invites us to put those beatitudes to work, to live the kingdom life now. Regardless of the persecution that will come, we are to live into the hope, comfort, and eternal life that is Christ Jesus.

Workers Ahead

Spend a few minutes defining "works righteousness." Search for a definition if you are unclear about it. Another way of looking at the issues of "works righteousness" versus "saved by faith alone" is to think of two different kinds of righteousness—passive and active. Based on Martin Luther's teachings, the Protestant church has often taken the "saved by faith alone" (passive) idea to the extreme, so that we have made our faith into something private and autonomous rather than serving our neighbors. Passive righteousness is in the relationship with God. We express our faith, and no works can produce salvation. Righteousness is a gift we receive from God.

If our passive righteousness is a personal faith where God saves us without our effort, the second type of righteousness is an active one. It is in regard to our relationship with other creatures—God's created beings. In response to God's gift of grace, we become active in our relationships with others. We are saved by faith alone, but we are to be active in serving our neighbor. These concepts can be a little confusing. After you have processed that explanation, spend some time quietly reflecting on the ideas.

As a class, write a litany, a prayer, or a dramatic reading based on the beatitudes. Use your imaginations to work together on ways you would like to see the beatitudes used in worship. When complete, share it with your pastor or worship team, and ask that it be used at an appropriate time during the year.

> How can our understanding of putting faith into action mistakenly become a "works righteousness faith"? How do we put our faith into action without falling into the belief that our good works will save us?

In the Rear View

Jesus' followers were largely those who are listed in the beatitudes: the poor in spirit, those who mourn, the pure in heart, and so forth. His message offered them comfort, hope, and eternal life, none of which they had found by adhering to the Law. The people saw the wisdom in Jesus' words.

Read Matthew 5:1-12 again. Talk with others in your group about the wisdom found in Jesus' words. How will you apply that wisdom to your life?

> How is your community of faith being called to minister to those whom Jesus mentioned? In what ways has your community of faith "blessed" the poor, hungry, meek, etc.? In what other ways could your faith community bless people who are in those situations?

Travel Log

Day 1:

Find a quiet place that is free from distractions. Slowly read Matthew 5:1-12. Sit silently as you listen for God to reveal to you the essence of your faith. Breathe deeply and in rhythm as you simply sit in the presence of God. After five minutes or so, write about your faith; describe the essence of your discipleship. Read through what you have written. Reflect on what surprised you about your own faith.

Day 2:

The lesson this week pointed out the difference between "believers" and "disciples." Reflect on those differences. In what ways are you a believer? a disciple? Do you agree that there is a difference? Write about those differences.

Day 3:

The first and eighth beatitudes end with the phrase "for theirs is the kingdom of heaven." What does that phrase mean to you? When you are ready, write or journal for a few minutes on your understanding of that phrase.

Day 4:

Jesus' sermon would have caused the disciples and others to re-examine their faith beliefs. Develop a bumper sticker statement that you think best represents your faith and beliefs (boiling down your faith).

Day 5:

As a disciple of Christ, in what ways do you think of yourself as a prophet? How does the scripture lead you to that conclusion? Make some notes as to the things about which you would prophesy.

Day 6:

Consider the ways you have persecuted others. Think imaginatively about what persecution can look like, and be honest with yourself and with God. Sit quietly, asking God to reveal the ways in which you have persecuted others because of their faith. Ask God to help you see these things and to forgive you. Write a letter through which you ask forgiveness from anyone whom you have persecuted. If you are not aware of a particular person or group you have persecuted, write a general letter regarding thoughts you may have had about other groups.

Day 7:

Make a list of the ways in which you have started applying the wisdom of Jesus' statements in your daily life. Which areas do you still need to address? Make a second list of ways in which you will address them.

www.ingramcontent.com/pod-product-compliance
Lightning Source LLC
Chambersburg PA
CBHW080937040426
42443CB00015B/3450